<u>Growing Up During the Great Depression</u>
How Neighborhood Families Survived

By
Edmond Theriault

Publisher
Brian J. Theriault / Theriault's Snowshoes   **Author / Edmond Theriault**
P.O. Box 242
Fort Kent Mills, Maine 04744 U.S.A.

www.Ilovesnowshoes.com
www.Northamericansnowshoes.com

theriaultsnowshoes@gmail.com

Book Layout © 2017 BookDesignTemplates.com

Growing Up During the Great Depression / Edmond Theriault -- 1st ed.
ISBN 978-0-9910069-4-6 soft cover-Perfect Bound
ISBN 978-0-9910069-5-3 / EPUB

012
Bibliographies of individual

Editor & Diagrams: Edmond Theriault
Technical Assistance: Tracey Hartt, Brian J. Theriault, Louise Latvis, Corinne Douglass, Laurie Theriault

Aroostook County, Maine, USA
Printed in the United States of America

Dedication: To my son, Galen Theriault and his wife, Bess.

Contents

Chapter 1
Introduction...4

Chapter 2
Food...18
    Buckwheat/Oats
    Potatoes

Chapter 3
Farm Animals...31

Chapter 4
Fishing/Hunting/Trapping..36

Chapter 5
Households..43

Chapter 6
Entertainment...56

Chapter 7
Health...64

Chapter 8
Government Programs..65

Chapter 9
About the Author..67

INTRODUCTION

The Great Depression created difficulties for almost all the people of Fort Kent, Maine. Most of the people were Frenchmen with a few Englishmen, and one Native Americans (Dennis' and Trombleys'). The French came from Nova Scotia and Quebec. Most of the Frenchmen had never gone to school. They had to learn to survive. They suffered many hardships and mistreatments in the war between France and England. The English came from downstate and seemed to have all the money to start businesses, especially cutting the virgin timber. We were thankful that our land and forest produced plants and animals to help us survive. My family and neighbors endured.

Photo taken about 1924 in front of Alexis Babin's combination house and store on South Perley Brook Road in Fort Kent Maine.

Bottom row: left to right, 1. Philomena Lozier Babin (Alexis Babin's wife) Born 1879- Died 1963 at the age of 84. 2. Leone (Michaud) Bouchard, Henry Michaud and Catherine Babin's daughter married to Emile Bouchard, Leone died on Nov. 15, 1987 at the age of 79. 3. Edna Dubois (Bouley), daughter of Paul Dubois and Laura Babin married to Rosaire Bouley on June 10, 1987 and died at the age of 65. 4. Catheine (Michaud) Desjardins daughter of Henry Michaud, married to Albenie (Bill) Desjardin. 5. Adrien Dubois son of Paul Dubois 6. Andre Dubois son of Paul Dubois 6. Andre Dubois son of Paul Dubois. 7. Mattie (Voisine) Saucier 2nd marriage to a Mr. Dunn. Daughter of Ben Voisine and Mattie Babin, married to Rene Saucier and 2nd marriage to a Mr. Dunn. 8. Alma (Dubois) Fitzgerald, daughter of Paul Dubois. 9. Jerry (Tidow) Michaud son of Henry Michaud. 10. Noah Michaud son of Raphael Michaud (Neighbor). Back row left to right: 11. Ludvine (Michaud) Boutot, Henry Michaud's oldest daughter, died Sept. 24, 1966. 12. Laura (Babin) Dubois wife of Paul Dubois. 13. Marie (Duguay) Babin second wife of John Babin, first wife of John Babin was Hermline Duguay sister of Marie. 14. John Babin (Jean Baptist) known as grandfather. 15. Ben Voisine husband of Mattie Babin. 16. Paul Dubois husband of Laura Babin. 17. Alexis Charette neighbor across the road. 18. Alexis Babin owner of general store.

I do not know how the land was divided and sold. During the depression, many families seemed to own small farms with wood for heat, space for animals. and a garden for food. It seemed like very few people had any money. They blamed President Hoover. That's where the buck stopped. That time was known as "The day of the dollar." Men who could find work put in twelve hours a day, from six a.m. to six p.m., for one dollar and no benefits.

The majority of houses being built were small. Almost all the houses were not insulated properly or not at all. Money was not available, so when winter came with snow and cold weather, the lost heat melted the snow on the roof and the water formed icicles on the lower edge of the roof. The icicles grew rapidly if the snow was not removed. This could create great danger from the growing icicles that sometimes almost reached the ground. On the roof, the ice would pile up. It was common to see men on ladders breaking the ice with an axe.

Most of the jobs available were given to family members or close friends. I do not remember when the Bradbury Mills was operating. They must have employed quite a large number of men. The mill was built over the river, below the dam used for power. The trees were brought to the mill in the river spring drive. The mill sawed all types of lumber. There was a section where they sawed cedar shingles and bunched them for shipping. Everything was piled near the railroad tracks for shipping. The sawdust and everything else that was not wanted went down the river.

(F) Inez, Rita, Gloria, Ethel
(B) Lillian, Kathleen, Lori Ann (Theriault)

South Perley Brook Road was a dirt road. In the winter, the road was not always open. One summer, before I was going to school, my cousin, Clarence Voisine and I were playing in the ditch. He had a toy horse and so did I. My iron horse had a leg missing, but it could still stand up in the dirt. Automobiles were not seen very often on the road and horse traffic was slow. I never figured out why my cousin, all of a sudden, decided to cross the road. He ran right in front of a car that was coming down the road and was carried/dragged over a hundred feet. One of the neighbors who witnessed the accident, ran and picked him up. I was sure that he was dead, so I ran crying to tell my mother. My cousin was not hurt too badly because, in a few days, we were again playing in the ditch.

The roads in Fort Kent were all dirt roads except for Main Street, which was made of concrete. During our long and cold winters, with its deep snow, there was only one way to make trails. You needed snowshoes to walk on top of the snow. After making two or three trips on a trail with snowshoes, the cold nights would freeze the trail so you could walk on it.

Edmond Theriault

Many residents kept a big dog and would get a dog harness and a sled to travel to get supplies and other needed items from the grocery store. Going downhill, the driver could ride, and going uphill he could help the dog. The German Shepherds seemed to be preferred. The dogs seemed to enjoy the job so much that when the driver picked up the collar of the harness, the dog would jump right in and was ready to go.

My grandfather had a small farm next to his brother Exiore. They each had a horse. When it came harvest time, they got the two horses together and formed a team to do the hard pulling. Harvest time was probably the happiest time of my young life. The relatives were all working together to store food for the coming winter. An added bonus was my grandmother's cooking. There was always plenty of sweets. I never heard anything about money, and I had nothing to worry about.

The house my mother inherited from her parents was a welcomed gift indeed. It still stands on its concrete foundation today. The house was two stories high and about forty feet square with an attached kitchen twenty feet by twenty feet on the west side. A woodshed about twenty feet wide by twenty-five feet long was attached to the kitchen. At the end of the woodshed was a barn, attached to the woodshed, but longer. The kitchen, the woodshed, and barn were lined up on the driveway side on the west. The barn was big enough for a horse, a cow, a pig and chickens. The hay was stored in the upper half story.

When my parents moved into my mother's parents' house, the kitchen had a separate dining room. It did not take long before the need for more eating space become apparent. They removed the wall between the kitchen and dining room and got a longer table and benches for two sides of the table. Most of the food was placed on the table and my father would serve the children. That eliminated the need to be constantly passing food around. We did not have to worry about lefto-vers, since I don't remember seeing any.

Inside the house, the first level floor was hardwood (maple). The second floor was tongue and grooved three-inch-wide soft wood. That was all that was finished on the second story until after World War II. The walls of the kitchen were finished with varnished hard pine. The remainder of the first story walls were finished with beaverboard with different colors for each room. There was no running water or bathroom until after World War II when the family moved back from Lewiston, Maine.

One Sunday in the summer, children in the neighborhood had gone to play on the hay. Someone had brought matches and set the hay on fire. The young ones come down in a hurry. The neighbors were all home when the alarm was shouted. Everyone came running with buckets of water. People were passing the pails of water to those on the barn where the fire was. I went into the barn to get our little pig out. He must have weighed about twenty pounds. He ran around his pen and did not want to get out. The smoke was getting thicker and I was having a hard time breathing. I knew I had to get out of there, so I grabbed that pig and carried him out. The fire was put out and the excitement was over. One of my younger brothers was missing and we found him hiding under the front porch. He admitted that he had set the fire.

It was at that time that my father decided to move the barn as far as he could on our lot. The outhouse was placed right before the barn, so we only need-ed to shovel snow for one path. The barn was covered with unpainted cedar shingles. The house was finished with clapboards and painted a light yellow with white trimmings.

Before electricity came to our road, we used a kerosene lantern and lamp. I have no idea how much kerosene cost, but when automobiles started showing up, the price of gas was twenty-five cents per gallon, and on special, it was five gallons for a dollar.

I don't know where the electricity came from, but when it came in the early 1930's, a meter was put on our house and one line brought the electricity to the kitchen for one bulb.   The first thing my mother wanted was a clothes washing machine, which she got. Every Monday she would roll the washer under the light bulb and connect it. The water had to be brought in in pails from the outside pump. If she needed hot water, a boiler was put on the wood stove to heat it. The washer had rubber rollers that were used to squeeze the water out of the clothes. I remember hearing about women getting fingers caught in between the rollers and their hands were badly damaged. Few women could read and follow instructions.

All the children went to the Baxter School, where we stayed until the eighth grade. Many children dropped out. We had plenty of paper and pencils and some books. My mother warned us that she did not want us to bring the books home. If we had homework, we had to do it in school. I believe she was afraid books could be lost. We all spoke French in school except the teacher. She was English. I did not want to speak English so there was not much communication between the teacher and the students.   I believe the main reason we were sent to school was to get us out of the house, especially in the winter.

All the children had a job to do around the house before going to school. As time would go on, our job would change depending on what had to be done. My mother was the inspector and it was hard to get away with anything. I don't remember anyone being punished except for some loud noise or being deprived of going somewhere. We were warned they did not want to hear complaints from our teachers, and we were to get passing ranks.

In the summer, we were told to go fishing or go pick berries, which were growing not too far from home. The wild strawberries came first, then raspberries and blueberries. We spent a lot of time fishing. Perley Brook was on one side of the house running west to the Fish River that was running north and south. There were plenty of fish at certain times in the summer. The most common were brook trout, white fish, and salmon (land-lock). The majority of people had gardens that required time. Families needed firewood for the winters that were long and cold. There was no money and no tools that would have sped up the process.

There was a telephone line on South Perley Brook Road, but we only connected after I started working at the Fort Kent Post Office in 1950. The first telephone was not what it is today. If you called, you could hear most of the telephones on the line being unhooked and many people got the latest news this way.

Alban Theriault

Big Lake Trout (34") caught in Eagle Lake Maine

Joseph Theriault

My father would tell stories that could last for months. He would tell us only a part of the story and then he would stop when we were getting interested and ask us to remember where he had stopped and send us to bed. The stories lasted a long time because he could use the same characters in all his stories.

We did not suffer from lack of news. We did not have newspapers or radios. We got our first TV when my oldest son Alvin was going to college in Fort Kent. He was trapping to pay his way, and he had some good years. I don't know how he did it, going to college full time, getting up early to check his traps, skinning his catch, and taking care of the furs at night. Some foxes were worth seventy dollars. For Christmas in about the mid nineteen seventies, Alvin bought the family our first TV. We did not have books except for sears catalogs and sales papers. They provided some reading, paper dolls for the kids, and other uses.

"TRAPPER JOE"
Joseph T. s/o Arsene T.
& Olive T.

CHAPTER 2

FOOD

Electricity had not come to our road, so the only way to preserve food was with salt. Quite a few businessmen would build sheds. In the winter, they would cut cakes of ice on the river and store them in the sheds covered with sawdust. In the summer, they would deliver the ice to their customers who had wooden insulated boxes in which they could keep food cool.

Buckwheat/Oats

Work on the farm was labor intensive. The farms all seemed to grow oats and buckwheat. The buckwheat flour was used to make pancakes, ploys, for any meal. Buckwheat was easy to grow and easy to freeze. It could not be planted too early. When it was ripe, the work began. The men used a scythe with a kind of cradle on it to cut the plants. They started early in the morning when the plants were wet with dew so the grain would not be shaken off during the cutting. Each man with a scythe would start cutting a strip about a yard wide next to each other and go around the field leaving the cut buckwheat in a neat narrow row with the grain on top. They kept going around the field until the dew was gone or the field was finished. The cut plants would be picked up at the right time by men with forks and placed in horse-drawn wagons with a rack and canvas on the bottom to save any grain that was shaken off.

Before threshing machines were available, the threshing/cutting had to be done by hand. The cut plants would be gently placed on canvas and hit with two pieces of a rounded stick tied end-to-end loosely with rawhide. The whole plants would be hit with the loose end until all the grains were off the plants. The straw would be removed and new plants with grain were added and pounded. The grain would be picked up and winnowed in the wind. The grain was ready to be taken to the gristmill to be grounded into buckwheat flour. If you trapped, the hulls, could be used to cover your traps and the remainder to feed the pigs.

Edmond & Pete Theriault

I have never made a buckwheat pancake, but I have eaten them for over ninety years. Our family ate them often, especial during the Great Depression. We usually ate them with butter or margarine. Since we had no money, we often had to find a substitute. We take a piece of salted pork and wash the salt off the pork. We would put it in a plate. We would use our knives to scrape that piece of pork and spread that on our pancake. It was a little salted, but good. We would eat pancakes with creton (pork spread). If it was sweets we wanted, we would put molasses in our plates and dip the rolled pancake in it. We used a lot of molasses, but I don't remember how much it would cost. At the store, the molasses came in huge barrels, and you had to bring your own gallon jug. Molasses cookies and cakes are still my favorite.

The oats were cut and tied in small bunches that could be stacked in the field. Once dry, the bunches would be brought to a threshing machine where the oats would be separated from the straw.

Eva Theriault

Eva Theriault canning jars

Edmond Theriault

Potatoes

Potatoes were used with almost any meal. Potatoes grew well and, in a short time, proved to be the favorite crop. In just about every kitchen, there was a container made of wood that was kept making potato yeast for baking bread and everything else that needed yeast. Water and potatoes were added to the container to keep the yeast supply up.

I have seen small farmers with hand diggers, digging potatoes by hand. They were using ash baskets and cedar barrels in harvesting. Huge bulls were tied to do the hauling, since they cost less to keep than horses. They proved to be not too reliable during the moose fly and horse fly season. When the flies started eating them, they would flee from the pests and break machinery, and sometimes they would be hard to bring back.

I remember is my grandfather and his brother, Exiore, who lived next door. Each had a horse and they joined force to harvest their potatoes with an old potato digger pulled by two horses. The potatoes were picked mostly by children. The men would hitch the horses to the wagon and haul the potatoes to store in their cellars.

Everyone really waited for the potato harvest. My father and older brothers would go pick potatoes in the center of Aroostook County where the farmers were paying more per barrel. I would be left to take care of the animals. We usually had a cow, a pig, and chickens.

I would pick potatoes for local farmers. When I would ask them for a job, they would say, "Come tomorrow morning, and if you're good, I'll keep you." The going pay was one dollar a day. The local farmers were short of storage, so we picked the bigger potatoes going one way. Coming back, we would pick the small potatoes and keep them in separate barrels. The small potatoes were stored in the barn for animal feed.

Farmers brought the potatoes to the house for storing. The surplus off the fields that they could not sell was brought to the house. People dug cellars under their houses, and in the middle of the floor, they put a trapdoor. They would roll the barrels through the house door and dump the potatoes through the trapdoor into the cellar. When they needed potatoes, they opened the trapdoor and took them out. I heard of people in crowded homes forgetting that the trap-door was open and falling in the cellar. Since cellars were often not too deep, it did not create much news.

People had to go to the cellar often since potatoes were in almost every meal. For breakfast, it was mostly home fries and in other meals, they would be boiled or baked. In between meals, for snacks, the potatoes would be sliced and cooked on the hot stove. My father always said that my mother knew how to make thirteen kinds of fricasseed potatoes.

When the railroad came in about the early 1900s, it opened the way to a larger market. Farmers were planting more potatoes and had the need for storage near the railroad tracks. Sometimes, it was difficult getting the potatoes to the shipping points near the railroad. A new industry was created; build storage houses near the railroad track. New potato storage buildings were built, and bins were rented to farmers. Labor was not costly, so many storages houses were being built.

One of my cousins, Lorenzo, who was about 16, and many other young men were hired for fifty cents a day. I am sure the carpenters were paid more. Lorenzo and I both worked at the Fort Kent post office after World War II. One day, Lorenzo's former employer came to the post office, and Lorenzo asked him if he remembered making him work for fifty cents per day. He said he remembered, but there was something he did not know. The employer said, "Almost every day, full grown men came to see me, and they were willing to work for food and a place to sleep. I could not keep them for fifty cents a day, so you had a job."

The potato house storage business did not last too long. Many of the small farmers could not afford to keep up with the expensive equipment that was being produced. The harvesters did away with thousands of potato pickers and the labor that was involved. The roads had improved, and huge trailer trucks were more convenient and cheaper since they could go to the farms to pick up the load and deliver it exactly where needed. Potato growers took over the business and workers moved away to find jobs. The railroad was left with moving wood products and fuel.

Spring Greens/Plants

There are edible weeds that make good soups and can be used as green vegetables or even in salads. The soup that is my favorite and that I have eaten all my life is made with "poulette grase" (lamb's quarters) and potatoes. That is a weed that grows in all our gardens, and we don't even have to plant their seeds. The weeds drop their seeds in the fall and no matter how cold the winter, the plants grow early in the spring. All these edible weeds make good soups and salads.

The first greens we ate in the spring were the dandelions that grew just about everywhere. I also learned to take advantage of the early dandelions that grew in our garden. We ate the leaves of wild turnips, which grew well around potato fields.

We ate fiddleheads that grew where the land was wet. My father brought me to where they grew in his special spot when I was about twelve or thirteen years old.   I have been picking fiddleheads there for eighty years, and still going. Where I was picking fiddleheads, there was a small ridge. Every spring, I could hear partridges drumming for hours. I always wanted to go see how they did that, but I was always too busy taking care of my fiddleheads.

During the Depression, when few jobs were available, whole families would gather wild strawberries, raspberries, and blueberries that grew almost every-where on farms. They grew where fires had been used to burn the weeds and branches after the useful trees had been salvaged. The container used to pick fruit most often was empty pails that came when you bought four pounds of lard.

Each family had a member who was selected to be the salesman. The sales-man would leave in the morning with four pails of berries and go from house to house in the richer part of town. The early berries sold for a better price, but that didn't last long. Blueberries sold for fifteen cents a pail or two for twenty-five cents. The berries had to be really clean with no green berries and no leaves or weeds. My salesman brother would sell each pail for fifteen cents and turn in fifty cents. The ten cents he kept was enough to go to the movies.

While waiting for harvest season, we would cut our firewood for the winter. My father would buy a section of wood the farmers wanted cut, and we would go cut it. Winters were long and cold. We had no money and no tools that could have sped up the process. I remember going in the beginning when I would only go to bring lunch, and then I would stay all afternoon. My father did not want me to use an axe or saw. All I did was move branches and pile small trees. In the evening, we would go fishing in Perley Brook and in the Fish River where fish were plentiful at certain times of the year.

With our productive garden, we developed a way where we could survive. Many people had gardens that required time. The manure, straw, and everything else the pig would not eat was placed in a pile to make some kind of compost for garden fertilizing. Almost any dish that was cooked included plants from the garden and beef or venison. A piece of fresh pork was added to the cooking vegetables to give it taste.

Joseph Theriault

Edmond Theriault

Hazelnuts/Beechnuts

Hazelnuts grew wild almost everywhere. My father, while trapping, would locate where there were the most and would pick hundreds of pounds in their picky covering. When he brought them home, we would spread them out in a shelter where they would dry and ripen. In the winter, we would peel them and crack the nuts to eat and to put in food. It gave us something to do during the long evenings. After the children were grown up enough, they would pick them, peel them, and sell them for ten cents a glass full. The hazel nuts were good sellers. Alongside of the roads, some children still sell glasses of nuts, but at a higher price.

Beechnuts matured later on hardwood ridges. On nice Sunday afternoons, grownups would bring sheets or blankets and spread them on the ground around the tree. The stronger men would take a sledgehammer and hit it against the tree, shaking the ripe nuts down on their sheets or blankets. They would move from tree to tree and gather beechnuts.

Many animals and birds ate the nuts. The bears would make a pile of leaves mixed with nuts. They would remove the nuts by shaking the leaves. The heavy nuts would slide to the ground where it was easier for them to eat.

I have picked beechnuts while hunting. A light rain would fall and form a crust on the snow. The nuts that fell stayed on the crust and tended to end up in the low spot where they were easy to pick. I don't know if this was caused by late spring frost, but some years the trees produced no nuts.

CHAPTER 3

FARM ANIMALS

In cold weather, many farmers and non-farmers who had sick animals or young newborns did not hesitate to bring them into the house to warm them up or until they got better.

Pigs

During the depression, many families were saved from severe hunger by their pig. At that time, we had no electricity, so we butchered our fat pig in the beginning of December when the weather was getting cold, and we had snow. The young pig had been bought in the spring and fed table scraps, cull potatoes, and weeds from our garden.

We had a local butcher who had a horse and sleigh to carry his tripod made of three poles and all the other equipment. He would tell us the time he would be at our house. In the local area, we did not skin the pig or burn the hair off with straw. In my hometown, the most common way to butcher a pig was to bleed the animal and save the blood to make blood sausage. To keep the blood from curdling, the butcher would put salt in the pail containing the blood. He stirred the blood until a ball formed with the material that caused curdling and threw that away. This prevented the blood from curdling. The blood could be kept until ready to use. The butcher would clean the small intestines to use as casings.

We left the pig skin on the fat and ate it on the bacon. You could skin the pig, but this was considered wasteful. The most common breakfast for working men consisted of slices of fat and home fried potatoes. Some people preferred the fat sliced thin and crisp, and others liked it better sliced thicker and not crisp.

When the butcher arrived, he would shoot the pig and save the blood to make blood sausages. Once the pig was bled, there were three ways to proceed. One was skinning the pig. In some areas, the people preferred putting straw on the ground and setting the straw on fire. The dead pig was rolled slowly on the burning straw until the hair and a thin layer of skin was burnt. This gave a good taste to the skin.

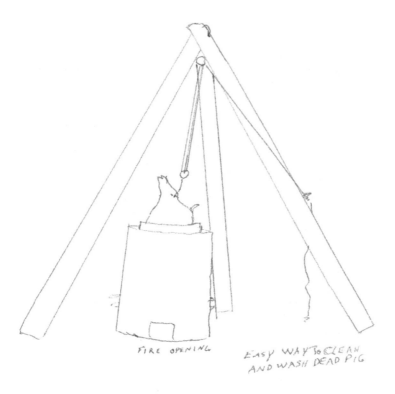

FIRE OPENING   EASY WAY TO CLEAN AND WASH DEAD PIG

The third and most common system was to hoist the dead pig by the hind legs and dip it in boiling water. We used a fifty-five-gallon metal barrel with an opening in the side bottom to make a fire to boil water in a smaller metal barrel suspended by pipes over the fire. There was no way of knowing the temperature of the water; there was no thermometer. The butcher tested the water by passing his hand in the boiling water. If it was too hot, he would add some cold water. He would set up his tripod of poles and pulleys over the boiling water. When the water was ready, he would not take much more than an hour.

The pig went in headfirst since that is the end that is the hardest to remove the hair off and clean. The butcher would test how the hair was coming off. After a short time, when he was satisfied, he would pull the pig out and put the back end in the hot water. While the back end was in the water, he would start cleaning the entire head. He would remove the hair and a thin layer of skin all over the head and the front end including the front feet. The nails on the feet, he would remove with a hook. He would then pull the pig out and finish cleaning the back end.

The butcher then would start cutting the pig open and saving the parts inside that were wanted by the owner. He would hang the pig up by the back feet and start removing the insides. All the fat inside the body would be saved and rendered to be used for cooking. The fat made doughnuts taste really good. The fat was preserved in salt in wooden containers or large jars to be used mostly in the summer. The parts to be used fresh were covered with snow and kept in wooden barrels where it was cold.

The small intestines were saved as casings for the blood sausage. The women would turn the intestines inside out and scrape the inside clean. They would wash them so they would be ready to be filled with the blood and whatever else they wanted to add. They used thread to tie the sausages any length they wanted.

The stomach would be emptied and later boiled with the remainder of the insides to get the fat out to be used to make soap. My mother always saved all the fat and grease to make a yellow soap. She would say that there was nothing that would clean wooden floors better.

The butcher removed the kidneys, the liver, the heart, the lungs, and the tongue. Every part of the pig that was not wanted would be boiled to get the fat out. Once it cooled, the fat would harden on the top of the water and be collected to make soap. Whatever was left was given to the chickens.

The butcher would saw the pig in two, lengthwise and leave the head hanging on one side. The sides were placed in a shelter where they could be cooled off. Once the meat had cooled off, we would cut it up and place it in a hardwood barrel with plenty of snow. We could keep it all winter where it was cool.

The head was used to make headcheese and creton. Creton is a spread, made of pork, that was very popular in this area. The spread could be used on toast, hot pancakes, or a snack when you were hungry. You could cut creton in small four-inch squares and freeze it for later use. The feet and ears were cooked and eaten. They were sticky, but good. The butcher would charge three dollars and move on to the next job. I do not think it would take two hours.

A custom developed before my time that was abandoned with the coming of electricity. During the summer, when a family had to butcher a pig for some reason, they would cut up the pig and send a "Morceau Du Voisin", piece for the neighbors. It was expected the neighbor would reciprocate at a later date. Many people had been saved from hunger or possible starvation. There were no safety nets for poor and older people.

Chickens

The chicken was helpful in keeping people from going hungry. The hens would be let loose early in the spring, and they would lay their eggs, sometimes well hidden. You would only see a hen occasionally when she showed up with a brood of chicks. Since she was not fenced, she managed to find food for her chicks until they were almost fully-grown. We would feed them cooked cull potatoes if feed could not be bought. The only way we could keep fresh meat was by keeping chickens alive until the cold weather arrived. Whenever visit would show up, we would be sure to have chicken stew with plenty of potatoes and dumplings in it.

A chicken was easy to prepare and cook, and the only fresh meat available during the warm weather. The chicken gizzard, the liver, the heart, the feet, and the feathers would be saved. The skinned feet of the chicken are sticky like pig's feet and tasted good. The small feathers would be washed, cleaned, and used in pillows. The larger feathers were used in fly tying for fishing. During trapping season, the remainder of the chicken was used for bait.

Rabbits

Some families raised rabbits for food. If they did not have a barn, they

would raise them in cages in require special food. They water. If you kept them in a they would eat anything that but I prefer the wild ones.

All the tree cutting for the land for planting crops duced mice and snowshoe trapping, he would bring food. When we brought a rab- mother would make a particu- dumplings, and other stuff.

the house. The rabbits did not seemed to do well on hay and pen outside in the summer, grew. I like domestic rabbits,

firewood and lumber opened and new growth that pro- rabbits. When my father was many snowshoe rabbits for bit home after hunting, my larly good stew with potatoes, That rabbit would make a meal for the family.

Rabbits are easy to trap. I don't believe I was more than 12 years old when I started trapping them. I caught a rabbit and cleaned it. An older couple who lived near home told me they would give twenty-five cents for a rabbit. I took it over, expecting they would be satisfied. The man said, "I will take this one, but don't bring any more." I asked why. He said, "You have wasted almost half of it. We save the kidneys, the liver, the heart, the lungs, and the head. If you want to bring us more, don't clean them. Bring them whole." I was happy to hear that I would get another chance.

Sheep

The meat of the sheep was good eating; and they did not require the best of pastures, since they seem able to do well on young trees. I have heard many complaints about domestic dogs getting together and running after sheep until they were hurt or killed. The bears also would get sheep for food on occasions. Sheep had to be kept where they were safe at night.

CHAPTER 4

FISHING/HUNTING/TRAPPING

My father was a fisherman, a hunter, and a trapper. All winter, we ate deer meat, rabbits, and fish.

Fish

Once the snow had melted, we ate a lot of fish from the Fish River and Perley Brook, mostly brook trout. We would go net smelting on Long Lake whenever we could get a ride. The smelts spawned in every brook around the lake, but I don't remember if there was a limit when we first started netting.

After the smelts had spawned, the suckers would come up the brooks to spawn. We caught plenty of suckers, but they had more bones, so we sold those to an older couple on the way home. They gave us twenty-five cents for about ten to twenty pounds of fish. I never went on fishing trips for suckers, but some farmers would get together with a horse and wagon and would bring back barrels of suckers. They would clean the fish and salt them. That was their fish for the summer. Salted ocean fish could be bought in Canada at a low price, but that cost money that we did not have.

Joseph Theriault

Squirrels/Chipmunks

Squirrels seem to hide nuts rather than store them. In the winter, they might forget where they are, so the nuts are left for seed. Chipmunks are different. They store all they can in different holes in the ground. Chipmunks stay in underground homes in the winter and are not seen until spring. I saw chipmunks, but I didn't know what they were doing.

One year, when the beechnuts were plentiful, I decided to look underground to see what it looked like in their home. First, I had to find the hole where they entered. I noticed that when they were going one way, they had their mouth full. The next time the chipmunk went by me, I watched for the last spot I had seen him, and I would move there.

The chipmunk was so interested in what he was doing that he just ignored me. The third time it passed by, I saw where his hole was. I was surprised because I was expecting to see a pile of escalation around his hole. There was not any dirt from the hole around the entrance. There only was a small hole that was hard to see.

I decided to dig it out with my bare hands. First, I cut a small pliable branch about four feet long and sent it in the hole as far as it would go. I started moving the dirt on top of the branch. The chipmunk came to see what I was doing, and then he took his nuts somewhere else. I kept moving the branch in the hole and removing dirt.

I had not gone ten feet when I came to where beechnuts were being stored. From what I could see, the chipmunk would bring a mouthful of dirt out to be deposited outside the tunnel where I could not see. Some dry leaves were brought in and placed around the nuts. I had a small pail about two quarts that I filled up with nuts to bring home. I don't believe this was a permanent home because I did not see any rooms.

Partridge

There were a lot of partridges in those days. The partridge mostly ate beechnuts, and they seemed to like them. When cleaning them, their craws were sometimes so full I thought they might burst.

While working in the woods one summer when I was fifteen, I spotted a partridge under some bushes. She was well camouflaged. The only thing I could see was the dark eye. I knew she was hatching eggs, so every morning, I was hoping to see the chicks around her. It didn't happen; I had missed it. All that was left in the nest was the eggshells.

One spring, while going through the woods to fish in one of my good spots, I saw a partridge dragging one wing and barely able to walk. I followed her, but only could approach her a certain distance. After a while, she just flew away. I realized that she had drawn me away from her chicks.

Another year, while walking in an old road, I saw this partridge doing the same act. I did not move and tried to see where the chicks were hiding. The mother had disappeared. After about fifteen minutes, I decided to leave when I thought I heard peeping like a regular chick. That mother came flying from some bushes right to my head. She was hitting me with her wings and her beak. I did not want to hurt her, so I bent down and hurried out of there. I did not see any chicks.

Other times, when the chicks were older, but still small, they could fly away short distances. It is sad that today they have almost disappeared, along with other creatures in our woods.

Deer

My father would go hunting for deer with friends since the deer were further and he didn't have transportation. When I was going to high school, he would bring me to help get the meat out of the woods.

One time when there was about six inches of snow, he brought me to show me how he skinned the deer on the ground and cut the meat. Once the deer was skinned, he used his axe to cut up the meat. He packed the two hind steaks in a knapsack, one the large end first and the other the small end first. That was my load.

I headed back out of the woods to the car. When I reached the car and removed the knapsack, I fell forward on all fours. I got up and fell again. I crawled into the back seat and waited. My father and his two friends came, and we left. When we got home, I got out and was okay.

*****

My father went into trapping in the early 1940s. He would wait until after the harvest. He had to walk or use snowshoes to set and visit traps. There were no coyotes or raccoons around until about the 1950's. The Canada Lynx had never been numerous. The beavers had been trapped out before my time. My father found out from the fur buyers in town that the price for prime red fox skins had gone up to forty dollars. The season was short, but the price for fur made it worth the effort.

There were many small farmers at that time who had grain fields that fed mice. Where the farmers lived outside of town, the mice were increasing rapidly and doing damage to the grain in the bins. Farmers started getting cats to live in the barns to take care of the mice in the barns and the houses also.

Mice are the favorite food for red foxes, but foxes also eat cats and chickens. Foxes are smart, and they could tell from year to year where farmers disposed their dead animals or unwanted parts. The foxes would travel from farm to farm to check their feeding spots. Red foxes, with no competition and plenty of food, were numerous. They had no predators to compete with them, so they increased in number until they became more of a nuisance.

1945-
Joseph Theriault

Some of the farmers would shoot them and let them go to waste. My father, who knew many of the farmers, had no problem getting permission to trap. When my father asked for permission, the farmers were so happy to have him get rid of that nuisance that they would invite him to eat with them and would give him rides whenever it was possible. When the snow came, my father had to use snowshoes.

I remember seeing him leave home in the morning when it was still dark, with his snowshoes. Some days he would go start checking his traps at the end of his line and work towards home when daylight came. He almost always had foxes to carry. On weekends, he would take a break, and would send my older brothers

1943- Joe Dubois and Joseph Theriault

to check his traps. It was hard work. Everything he would catch had to be skinned that night. The foxes had to be skinned with the toes and claws and all the fur and head left on, since they were used for mounting.

The following years, my father joined a cousin, who was a good skinner but could not travel far on snowshoes. That proved more favorable. After a few seasons, everyone who could was trying to catch foxes, and the high prices disappeared. Some of those beautiful prime red foxes would bring twenty dollars. That kind of money was more than welcomed before winter and Christmas.

My father explained to me where foxes were more likely to pass in winter when was where there was more than six inches of snow. He showed me the unique way foxes traveled. They take steps in a straight line about four to five inches apart with the back feet stepping in the tracks made by the front paws. If they decide to come back, all they have to do is step in their tracks and the trail is already broken, saving energy.

Any other foxes going that way can just get in the tracks and the going is easy. Where many foxes have passed, the tracks only show one set of tracks going one way. As more foxes use the same holes to walk in, the holes get slight- ly enlarged. It takes a sharp eye to tell the difference. If you follow a fox tracks, you can be surprised to find tracks leav- ing or joining in every way.

CHAPTER 5

HOUSEHOLDS

Before electricity came to our backcountry, we would use kerosene lanterns and lamps for light. Many families made mattresses with a cotton container the size needed to fill with straw and oats. Changing the straw was easy and free. Beds could be made of round or split wood. Any time buildings had to be destroyed, whatever could be reused was saved, including the nails. The nails would be straightened with a hammer on a block of hardwood. Nails with rust on them held better than slick new nails. Saws to cut wood were homemade.

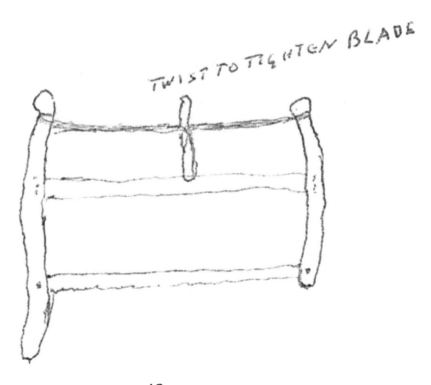

TWIST TO TIGHTEN BLADE

CUT TREE

PUT FOOT ON TREE TO STEADY

Clothing

Warm clothes were necessary in winter. The women had to do the sewing and washing of clothes by hand. My mother would buy us two pairs of overalls for fifty cents per pair to save our clothes. No material was thrown away. If a piece of garment could not be passed down to someone, it would be taken apart and made into something else. Small pieces were used for blankets and strips would be used to make rugs. Most of the house floors were made of soft wood. Where the traffic was heavy, as in doorways, the hard knots soon stood out if the floor was not protected with rugs.

Sheep produced the wool that kept people warm during the cold winters. Almost all the women could take care of the wool and knit almost all types of warm clothes. They could cover damaged pieces or take it apart and knit something else. The wool could be reused many times.

In the fall, after the harvest season, the families had earned a few dollars that they used to buy flour, sugar, beans, and items they would need for the winter. The flour was available in one-hundred-pound cotton bags, and other products also came in cotton bags. These empty bags were unsewn and used to make undergarments.

Electricity

Before electricity came to our road, we used a kerosene lantern and lamp. I have no idea how much kerosene cost, but when automobiles started showing up, the price of gas was twenty-five cents per gallon. On special, it was a dollar for five gallons. When electricity came, we had little money to spend on this luxury.

The dam on the Fish River that produced the power to run the Bradbury Mills broke. Electricity came to Northern Maine, so the mills were moved closer to the standing timber, eliminating the need for the spring drives on the Fish River from Eagle Lake, Maine. I don't know where the electricity came from, but when it came in the early 1930's, a meter was put on our house and one line brought the electricity. When electricity came to our street, we had one line put in the kitchen for one bulb. Later we got an extension cord to put another light bulb in the cellar.

The first thing my mother wanted was a washing machine since she had to do the washing by hand for her growing family. Every Monday, she would roll the washer under the light bulb and connect it. Then hang it to dry outside. We had to pump the water outside in pails and bring it in when needed. Some people would get their water from springs or the neighbor's pump. If she needed hot water, a boiler was put on the wood stove to heat it. The washer had rubber rollers that were used to squeeze the water out of the clothes. I remember hearing about women getting fingers caught in between the rollers and their hands being badly damaged. Few women could read and follow instructions.

Winter Survival

When men went to work in the woods in winter, some family members or friends would decide to close their homes and live together while their husbands were gone. Most of the time, they would go to the home that was the most convenient or had a place to bring their animals. In certain cases, water would be harder to get, so they put barrels for each family near the door. Each family would put snow in their barrel to melt for water to do their washing and for their animals. Unless they had enough animals in the barn to keep it warm, everything put in there would freeze solid. Each family would make their own food, so they would take turns with the stove and table. They would get together and get large containers of drinking and cooking water from springs or from neighbors.

My parents had fourteen children. We needed food for about twelve every meal at that time, counting our parents. (Some of the younger ones were not yet born.) In the winter, we had farmers store potatoes in our cellar. For the cellar storage use, we could use all the potatoes we needed. Potatoes were the only fresh vegetable we had all winter. Early in some fall seasons, we had some apples as our fresh fruit.

Hay

One summer, we had to go to the farm to help during haying. My father, Uncle Arthur Deschaine, and I had been working to bring hay in the barn. When we stopped to come in for supper, a lightning storm broke out. My aunt had started to cook on the wood stove. When lightening hit the top of the stove, my aunt said she was staying away from the stove until it was over.

We could see lightening everywhere as we watched in the window facing Exiore's house. About five hundred yards away, we saw lightening hit his chimney. Bricks went flying and smoke started coming out. Someone said we better go help. We grabbed some pails near the outside pump and started running in the road.

I had never seen anything like that. Lightening shot in every direction on the road as we ran. When we got there, nobody was home, so we went in. The flue collar/connection on the chimney had blown out and made a mess of soot everywhere. My father and uncle told me to put water in the pails while they ran up to the attic. My uncle helped my father get in the attic where the fire was. We passed pails of water to my father as he put out the fire. I do not know how much damage was in the attic, but there was black soot everywhere in the house.

The hay would be cut by a machine pulled by horses. It was left to dry on the field. Once it was dry, workers would load it by hand with forks on the wagon with a rack. They would bring the hay to the barn for storage. To unload the hay, they would use a rope and pulley that ran on a track at the highest part of the barn. A hay fork would be stuck in the load of hay and locked. The load would be lifted by a horse and moved to where it would be stored. The man unloading the hay had a smaller rope attached to the hay fork. He would unlock the hay fork and drop the hay where he wanted it.

Trees

Keeping warm in the long winters was one of the jobs that required much time. A section of trees from a farmer who wanted to expand his cultivated area was unbelievably cheap. Trees had to be cut and brought home with horses. That was not expensive when there was nothing else for the horses to do. Once the trees were home, they had to be cut with a homemade bucksaw into firewood about sixteen inches in length.

There were no chainsaws. The cut wood had to be brought into the wood-shed and piled. That woodshed was attached to the house so you would not have to go outside to get firewood during the winter. We would use about eight cords per year. It had to be handled about seven or eight times before it was put in the stove. Kindling had to be drier and split finer to light the stove with the help of paper.

Driving lumber was a dangerous business. The water was cold and so was the weather. There was a saying that the little Frenchmen in the St. John River Valley were the absolute best drivers because they could not swim. On long drives a long wooden boat was used for the cook, his kitchen, and equipment, which stayed behind the drive. Workers ate three meals a day, mostly pork and beans. At night, they would put a canvas on the ground and a second canvas for cover. The men would all crawl under, fully dressed until morning. The last drives on the St. John River were in the early 1950's.

The trees could be brought to the mills with horses, but the majority was brought by water. The men would cut the trees in the winter. They were piled on top of a steep bank near water or piled on the ice if it was strong enough. When the water was high in the spring as the snow and ice melted. The wood was already in the water or easy to push in the high water. Each company marked their trees and tied them to keep logs together on the lakes.

Ed & Joseph

1942-Ed, Eli, Stanly & Joseph

Eli

Joseph

~ 49 ~

Eli

Ed, Stanley, & Joseph

Ethel, Ed &Stanley

Lillian & Eli

Joseph

To keep trees together, they tied trees together using boom chains. Holes would be made about three inches in diameter in the ends of trees. The chain had a six-inch ring at one end and a piece of iron half an inch thick, about two inches wide, and about six inches long with a hold in the middle that would hold the pipe of metal balanced. The piece of iron would be passed down both trees and this would be continued with other chains and trees until the boom would go around the logs that were in the water. Even if the lake got rough, the trees were kept together.

The chains had to be taken off to go down river. To take the boom apart, you turned the logs and sent the metal piece back through the holes while holding the ring. When the chain had been saved and brought ashore, they were ready for the next time it was needed.

The summer I was a junior in high school, my father brought me and my younger brother Stanley into the woods of Monticello, Maine, about one hundred miles from home. We had to walk on a very rough road to a wood camp. The road was used to bring supplies to camp with horses and a big wagon. The melting snow and spring rain had made the road almost impassable.

The camp was near a good spring with plenty of water for the horses and a few pigs. On both sides of the length of the camp were the bunk beds. The bunk beds were made in two levels of solid boards. Each level was separated by a board of about six inches wide every four feet and seven feet long. You would get in from the foot of the bed from the middle aisle of the camp. That area was where you slept and kept everything you owned.

In the center aisle was a wood stove. A door was at the end of the center aisle that led into the dining room where the tables were. At the door entrance was a wide shelf with wash basins and pails of water for washing and drinking. Metal cups were hung on nails. You had to bring your own towel. On the other side of the door opening was the cook room with a stove and the utensils needed for preparing food. That was also an area where supplies were kept.

Another building was where the horses, hay, and oats were kept. The horses were tied in their stalls. At the entrance on the right was a latrine made of poles that you could sit on. There was also a shelter to keep the firewood in.

We had to walk about a mile to get to where we were cutting wood. We had to bring our axes and a crosscut saw to drop the trees and two metal four-foot bucksaws. We also had to carry our lunch prepared by the cook. Our working tools, we left where we worked unless the saws needed sharpening.

We were working piecework by the cord. Four feet by four feet by eight-foot-long piles. We peeled the trees as long as the sap was running. You could leave the bark on for lower pay. My father told us we could only cut and peel until the sap stopped running. Then we would get a horse and pull the peeled trees where we could cut them into four-foot lengths and pile them. The trees, by that time, were not as slippery and easier to handle.

The summer of 1940, my father, brother, and I worked at a logging camp in Monticello, ME. Mr. George Russell of Fort Kent was the boss of that camp and everything ran smoothly considering there were eight-two men working there. The food was adequate. There were no bathrooms, but that did not bother us too much because nobody that we knew had a bathroom at home. I only took my shoes off when I went to bed. After a short time, the straw moved to the sides of the bed, and I slept on the boards in the center. I never asked my father how much we were paid, and he never mentioned it. The scaler would measure how many cords of wood we had cut, piled, and marked. My father received the check.

We stayed in the woods until we had to come home for the start of potato picking and school. We made more money picking potatoes. Picking potatoes paid seven cents per barrel (180 lbs.). If you picked a hundred barrels, you made seven dollars. It was a great improvement from one dollar per day. If you could not help loading your barrels in the wagon, you had to pay one cent each to have it done. When I started picking for my father, he loaded all the barrels.

Henry Deschaines, one of the men from Fort Kent, told me that, one winter, he was in the woods with my father. He said the camp was near a fairly large pond because they needed water for the horses and men. My father had found out there were a great deal of brook trout in the pond, averaging about one pound each. He brought a pail full one Sunday and the men liked the fish. He was hired to fish and hunt.

My father thought it was easier to fish than hunt, so he was doing more fishing. Henry said, after a while, the boss told your father to slow down on the fishing. "The men are so sleepy; they have a hard time staying awake." (I don't know how true it is, but many people say eating fish makes them sleepy.)

ENTERTAINMENT

Playing Cards

Our grammar school would close during the months of January and February. We lived about one mile from the school. It was cold and sometimes the roads were not open, making it hard for the lower grade students get to school. With many people not working, neighbors gathered to play cards.

The most popular game was called 'Charlemagne'. People would learn to play at an early age, and everyone could choose a partner, playing against another set of partners. The losers would give their seats to other partners when they were available. Only the high cards from seven to the ace were used. Each player got eight cards. You got one chance to bid each game and teams scored points. The team won when they accumulated twenty-one points. Even today, when we meet, it is our favorite card game.

Five card stud was popular with older people. Since money was not available, some people would play for matches. Some would play for peppermints. As time went on, you could see the white peppermints turn brown. The most popular token in the end was wrapped small pieces of candy that sold really cheap. As conditions improved, you started seeing pennies in the game. There was a limit of one to two pennies. Other games were played, but they were not popular in my area.

Dancing

Dancing was quite popular. Some men and some women would dance alone. I did not dance, and I didn't know what they called it. My grandmother played an accordion for dancing, especially for young people. Quite a few of the men could play the harmonica and many could sing popular songs. I noticed that some of the men who were asked to sing always sang the same song. I suppose a regular song is always nice to hear.

My father was one of the few who could sing all the songs he had heard. He would sing folk songs about neighbors or people he knew. Professor Roger Paradis of Fort Kent University brought a tape-recorder to my father and asked him to tape all the French songs that he knew. He taped two hundred and seventeen songs. Whenever we would see my father and talk about his taping, he would think about other songs he had not taped.

My father was also a storyteller. When my father was telling stories, depending on the circumstances, he could bring smiles to the faces of his listeners, or he could bring tears to their eyes. He tried to tape French stories, but he said he could not. I believe he needed an audience to gauge responses.

Master Traditional Snowshoe Maker
Edmond Theriault

Snowshoeing

For the outdoors people, snowshoeing was available. My father had a pair that was made by his uncle. Many people made snowshoes during the depression. Willie Roy of Fort Kent was one of the last snowshoe makers. When I started thinking of retiring, my sons were hunting and trapping in the winter, and they needed snowshoes. I was hoping someone would see the need to keep this old Maine tradition from disappearing and start making them. I was planning on retiring at fifty-five years of age and I had only about three years to go. It was in January, with plenty of snow, when I asked my sons if I should try making snowshoes before I retired. They thought it would be great since they needed them.

The first thing I did was visit Willie Roy, who was getting along in years. He was glad to see that I was interested. He told me that he was in the process of stopping, and he gave me two strips of black ash that he was not going to use. We talked about the many people who made snowshoes before and during the depression. He said that most of them involved different members of the family. One would work on the frames, one would work on the rawhide, and one would do the weaving. Both men and women were involved. When someone would move, the others did not know how to do his job, so the project was set aside for other work.

Willie was the only one in his family who had learned all the different steps. He told me that one winter, his family had made one hundred pairs of snowshoes. I asked him how much they were getting per pair. He said they were selling for two dollars a pair with the harness. He showed me every tool they were using for different jobs. The majority of the tools were handmade from discarded metal and wood. He told me that if I ran into problems to come and see him. He was helpful in getting me started.

I have now worked on snowshoes for over forty years. My son Brian, who has been with me all this time, is left to teach others the traditional way of making snowshoes. He is the one who insisted we write the book "Leaving Tracks" to make it easier for others to follow us in making snowshoes. He is the one who took all the pictures and made all the diagrams included in the book.

After getting our first tree and our first cowhide, we got down to work. The first pair was tested by my oldest son Alvin, who was trapping beavers to pay for his college. He would leave early and get home late in the evening, dragging up to four beavers. He would drag carcasses downstream, but sometimes he had to drag uphill, so he had to make two trips going up. When he would get home, the first thing I did was examine his snowshoes to see how the snowshoes were taking the stress. Alvin weighed one hundred eighty pounds and pulling these beavers was a good test for the rawhide. I had to change the way of tying the rawhide so it would not move. If the rawhide moves, it means that it will be loose somewhere and not have the same bounce.

Skis

A cousin of my mother asked father to bring him a beech tree, and he would make us some skis. The skis came out very well, and they lasted quite a few years. They were made with a hole under the foot where you could pass a leather strap that would buckle on top of the foot.

Sleds

We made sleds for riding, moving wood, and other moving tasks. We made two runners about four feet long using boards five-inch-wide and one inch thick, shaped in the front for sledding. Two strips of hardwood, one half inch thick and a good two inches wide were nailed centered under the runners. The runners were nailed together with a piece of board sixteen inches wide. The hardwood strips would be steamed for bending.

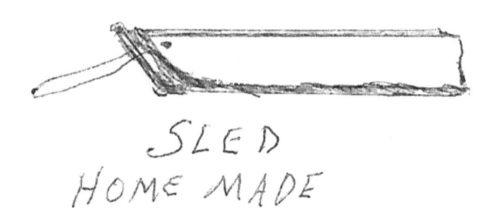

SLED
HOME MADE

We also made what we called "bubs" for sliding; it was made from a hardwood stave from a wooden barrel. A piece of firewood of the right height was nailed slightly back of the center of the stave. A piece of board was nailed on top to sit on the post. The post was braced on both sides on the stave. You rode sitting and controlling with your legs and body.

BUB

CHAPTER 7

HEALTH

During the beginning of the depression, there were few doctors around, except in Canada. The sick people depended on midwives or ordinary people who knew how to use plants. My father would tell me the French names of the different plants and what they were used for. Sometimes he would bring different plants for his mother who used them to treat sick people. I had never been sick, so I could not see why I needed them.

My wife Joan's grandmother, Henriette Pelletier, was a midwife and has been credited with helping bring over 500 babies into this world. There was a doctor in Canada, but the women preferred Henriette since she had experience and never charged anything. Most of the time, the people would be able to come and get her with a horse. But if the road was not open, she would get on her snowshoes and go. Almost everyone had snowshoes. They came in handy around the house, and if you had to go in the woods for any reason, they were absolutely necessary.

CHAPTER 8

GOVERNMENT PROGRAMS

President Franklin Delano Roosevelt came into office during the worst of the depression in 1932. Few people had jobs, and money was scarce. Men working in the woods could not really support their families. Some farmers, who needed help, would take young unmarried men for their keep. It was during the President Franklin Delano Roosevelt's administration that programs were started to put people to work. That was about the mid 1930's.

It was at this time the government came up with the Work Progress Administration (WPA) Program. The program was created to put men with families to work. In the winter, the men would cut firewood for town and disabled use. They had a camp in the woods where men would go for five days a week to cut firewood that the town would deliver to the people who needed it. The trucks that transported the men were not heated and cold. Some of the men would take short-cuts on snowshoes though the woods to work or to be picked up by the truck closer to camp. In Fort Kent, the WPA put in the first sewer system in the town of Fort Kent. They made many roads passable for vehicles and also built new roads. The men would be paid a salary of $45.00 a month.

The Civilian Conservation Corps (C.C.C.) program was for young men who were unemployed and not married. They lived in camps and were organized similar to the military. They wore uniforms and had ranks. They built roads and worked in parks. I do not remember exactly, but I think they were paid about fifteen or eighteen dollars per month. In our schools, we often spoke French. This program served these young men of Fort Kent area well by giving them an opportunity to learn to speak and understand English. It also helped them to learn how the military worked. It was not long before World War II came and the young men were drafted. I believe most of them ended up going in the military service. This program left me the only guy in the eighth grade to go to Baxter High School.

Another program had free seeds to plant a garden. Later, pressure cookers were installed, and cans were used to can the vegetables. The people would bring their vegetable to the cannery and they would receive half of the cans. The cans of vegetables were used to pay the people who worked at the cannery. The left-over canned vegetables would be given to the people who could not work. I believe the town was in charge of most of these programs. They could exchange their surplus with other communities for other types of surplus.

Our way of life was improving. When my father worked on WPA, he was getting paid $22.50 twice a month. When he started work where he could bring my older brothers, that made our life even easier. In the fall during harvest, everyone who could pick potatoes was in the field. We were paid seven cents per barrel (180 lbs.). A picker who could pick 100 barrels in a day made $7.00. There were potato storage houses near home, and when they had to load railroad boxcars at night, they would ask me to work. The pay was 35 cents an hour.

CHAPTER 9

ABOUT THE AUTHOR

Edmond Theriault was born on March 22, 1923 in Fort Kent, Maine. He was the fourth son of Eva and Joseph Theriault. They raised a family of fourteen children during the Great Depression (1929-1939) and World War II (1939-1945).

Edmond's mother was proud of her large family and said she would rather have her sons fighting for her than anyone else. All the boys in the family served in the military during World War II. Eli joined the Army Air Corps, went to flight school, and was made a B-17 pilot. Alban joined the Infantry and spent one and a half years as a platoon leader in Europe. Edmond joined the Army Air Corps, went to flight school, and spent twenty-two months in the Pacific Theater as a B-17 pilot. Alire (Pete) joined the Air Force. Donald served for over thirty years in the Air Force.

Joseph & Eva Theriault

Eli & Edmond & Alban Theriault

Pete Theriault

Stanley & Edmond Theriault

CPSIA information can be obtained
at www.ICGtesting.com
Printed in the USA
BVHW052029300421
606133BV00013B/1938